YOUR KNOWLEDGE HAS VALUE

- We will publish your bachelor's and master's thesis, essays and papers

- Your own eBook and book - sold worldwide in all relevant shops

- Earn money with each sale

Upload your text at www.GRIN.com
and publish for free

Tobias Hollarek

Overview of RGBD-SLAM Approaches

GRIN Verlag

Bibliografische Information der Deutschen Nationalbibliothek:

Die Deutsche Bibliothek verzeichnet diese Publikation in der Deutschen National-
bibliografie; detaillierte bibliografische Daten sind im Internet über http://dnb.d-
nb.de/ abrufbar.

Imprint:

Copyright © 2012 GRIN Verlag GmbH
Druck und Bindung: Books on Demand GmbH, Norderstedt Germany
ISBN: 978-3-656-54634-4

This book at GRIN:

http://www.grin.com/en/e-book/264677/overview-of-rgbd-slam-approaches

GRIN - Your knowledge has value

Der GRIN Verlag publiziert seit 1998 wissenschaftliche Arbeiten von Studenten, Hochschullehrern und anderen Akademikern als eBook und gedrucktes Buch. Die Verlagswebsite www.grin.com ist die ideale Plattform zur Veröffentlichung von Hausarbeiten, Abschlussarbeiten, wissenschaftlichen Aufsätzen, Dissertationen und Fachbüchern.

Visit us on the internet:

http://www.grin.com/

http://www.facebook.com/grincom

http://www.twitter.com/grin_com

Overview of RGBD-SLAM Approaches

Hauptseminar Computer Vision & Visual Tracking for Robotic Applications SS2012

Tobias Hollarek

Lehrstuhl für Echtzeitsysteme und Robotik

Fakultät für Informatik

Technische Universität München

Abstract

In this paper I will introduce the reader to RGB-D SLAM which has become the focus of interest for many researchers lately. This is due to the development and distribution of cheap RGB-D sensor devices such as the Microsoft Kinect. After an introduction I will present which steps have to be taken to implement a working SLAM system using RGB-D data. In section three I will introduce three different approaches and will present how they implemented the SLAM and what they did to increase speed, accuracy and robustness of their algorithms. I will then compare the results of all approaches. In the next section I will present what optimization methods two of these approaches implemented to improve their mapping by optimizing with a global approach. These implementations also are reviewed and compared as far as that was possible. In section five I will present how two different approaches store the mapping after all calculation is done in a sophisticated and compact way. Finally I will conclude over the results I collected and give an outlook on possible future developments.

Index Terms

RGB-D, SLAM, ICP, RANSAC, loop closure, Kinect

CONTENTS

I. INTRODUCTION

Simultaneous Localization and Mapping (SLAM) is a technique that has been used in robotics and many other applications for quite some time now. One important application is when robots are placed in an unknown environment. In that case they do not have any data to orient themselves. They do not know their position within the setting nor do they know anything about the setting itself. Therefore a method is required which is able to simultaneously build a map of the environment and localize the robots position within this map. That is exactly what SLAM provides. To do so SLAM needs depth information of the surroundings. These were traditionally acquired using laser scanners, which usually provide depth information over long distances with quite small errors. They also usually cover a large angle of view, which helps a lot when performing SLAM.

Fig. 1. Example dataset of RGB (left) and depth values (right) of a Microsoft Kinect. The darker the pixel the closer it is. White space contains unidentified distances [1]

The downside of using laser scanners on the other hand is, that these systems usually are quite expansive. Also they can only provide a depth map of the surroundings. To incorporate color information into the produced map at least one RGB Camera is needed. Some systems only use stereo RGB Cameras and calculate the depth information from their pictures together with the knowledge of the relative position of the two cameras. This approach though needs a lot of extra calculation and still is not very accurate. RGB-D SLAM combines these two approaches to produce colored 3D maps of unknown environments using both: RGB and depth values for a large number of pixels. It has recently become a field of great interest due to consumer devices such as the Microsoft Kinect which provide color and depth information at a relatively low price.

This makes it possible to give access to working SLAM systems to a much larger group of people such as research groups with low funding, students or even consumers. One has to keep in mind though that the data provided from such low cost devices usually is not as exact as the data from expensive high resolution laser scanners. This means that RGB-D systems can either be used for learning purposes since the underlying software is similar to, if not exactly the same as with more exact systems. But Kinect style devices for RGB-D SLAM can also be used in applications where the result does not have to be very exact. In the following essay I will present the basic steps a RGB-D SLAM system takes to create a map of the surrounding and localize itself within that surrounding. Then I will present three approaches from different research groups and analyze what they have in common and where they differ from one another. I will then evaluate the performance of these approaches concerning real time calculation, robustness and precision as far as that is possible from the data provided in the sources.

II. RGB-D SLAM

RGB-D SLAM can be divided into two basic steps. The first one is the pose estimation and frame alignment, where a first approximation of the surroundings and the trajectory of the device within it is calculated. After that usually a global optimization is performed which improves the first mapping using additional constraints.

A. pose estimation and frame alignment

In this step, or rather these two steps, the actual SLAM is performed. Since it is *simultaneous* localization and mapping these two usually independent problems here are connected even on implementation level. That is why I will handle them within one chapter and compare the combined approaches.

The goal of this step is to build a map and localize the robot within that map. Since neither map nor localization is given at the start usually one just initializes a coordinate system with the robots location at the origin. The map then gets build around that position into the coordinate system. To do so the data points (color and depth values of each pixel) of one frame are mapped to the corresponding data points in the following frame. This does mean that this technique only does well if a large part of the two images has the same content. This leads to the constraint, that the camera cannot move too fast since then two succeeding frames are far apart and pose estimation and frame alignment get a lot harder. Still: With the knowledge of corresponding data points the new image can be correctly aligned with the old data to augment the map that has been produced up to this point of time. From corresponding data points a transformation can be calculated which represents the shift of the first picture to the second one. From this shift the movement of the robot can be estimated and a new position is calculated by applying the transformation to the old position of the robot. These two steps have to be done for every image the RGB-D camera provides to get the best result possible in both pose estimation and mapping of the environment.

2

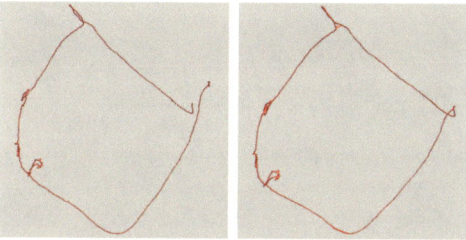

Fig. 2. loop closure detection and correction from a real example [1]

B. global map alignment

Usually different approaches to SLAM all include different optimization techniques to produce their results more efficiently, more robust, easier or more exact. One optimization that nearly all approaches include is the optimization of the created map on a global scale. Usually the change of the pose of the robot from one frame to the next can not be computed exactly. Also images can usually only be aligned within some uncertainty. Therefore after a long running time the constructed map may vary a lot from the real world. To improve this estimation a very common approach is to implement a loop closure detection. This algorithm compares every new frame with the map that has been created so far and checks if the scenery observed right now is already somewhere in the map. The robot does store its position and should therefore know if he gets to the same position twice. But since small errors occur in each frame alignment these can accumulate to form misalignments that are too big for the robot to notice that it actually is at the same spot again. For that reason this has to be checked by comparing images and not the internal locations. If a loop closure is detected and the estimated internal position of the robot (and the map) is not correct a global realignment is performed where the active position gets set to the older position and everything in that loop gets realigned accordingly. With this improvement even large maps can be created without having to worry about giant errors piling up since they can easily be minimized by producing a loop closure. The result is a globally consistent alignment of the complete data set.

III. POSE ESTIMATION AND MAP ALIGNMENT

In this chapter I will introduce the reader to three different RGB-D SLAM systems and compare their performance concerning efficiancy, robustness and exactness. The first approach I will introduce is from Henry et al. [1]. This team of researchers implemented a working RGB-D SLAM system using a Kinect style camera to perform "dense 3D modeling of indoor environments" [1]. To optimize their system they have developed many features that improve the standard algorithms to get better approximations and performance. The second system is from Enders et al. [2]. They also base their implementation on a Kinect camera but differ in some features from Henry et al. Also they try to introduce a better comparison throughout different RGB-D SLAM systems by evaluating their implementation on a publicly available data set. This allows other researchers to compare the performance of their systems under exactly the same circumstances. The third team [3] uses a technique for frame alignment which differs greatly from the other two and therefore makes it interesting to compare with.

All the approaches use a Microsoft Kinect or a Kinect style camera which all have about the same hardware features:

- 640x480 pixels each containing RGB and depth information
- 30 frames per second
- a depth range of about 5m
- a camera angle of 60 degrees
- relatively noisy depth measurements of about 3cm uncertainty at 3m distance

A. RGBD-ICP from Henry et al. [1]

As all the approaches that i will present here the system from Henry et al. [1] produces rich 3D maps of indoor environments containing depth and color information. The authors divide their system into three main components:

- spatial alignment of consecutive data frames
- detection of loop closure
- globally consistent alignment of the complete data

In this chapter we will concentrate on the first of these three. The whole procedure that Henry et al. used for their SLAM is schematically shown in Fig. 3.

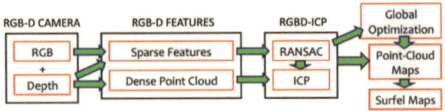

Fig. 3. Overview of the steps of RGB-D SLAM as implemented by Henry et al. [1]

input : source RGB-D frame P_s and target RGB-D frame P_t

output: optimized relative transformation T^*

1   $F_s \leftarrow$ Extract_RGB_Point_Features (P_s);
2   $F_t \leftarrow$ Extract_RGB_Point_Features (P_t);
3   $(T^*, A_f) \leftarrow$ Perform_RANSAC_Alignment (F_s, F_t);
4   **if** $|A_f| < \gamma$ **then**
5 | $T^* = T_p$;
6 | $A_f = \emptyset$;
7   **end**
8   **if** $|A_f| \geq \phi$ **then**
9 | **return** T^*;
10 **else**
11 | **repeat**
12 | | $A_d \leftarrow$ Compute_Closest_Points (T^*, P_s, P_t);
13 | | $T^* \leftarrow$ Optimize_Alignment (T^*, A_f, A_d);
14 | **until** *(*Change $(T^*) \leq \theta)$ **or** *(*Iterations > MaxIterations*)* ;
15 | **return** T^*;
16 **end**

Fig. 4. The RGB-D ICP algorithm used in Henry et al. [1]

The part that I want to concentrate on for now is the RGB-D ICP Algorithm, which is described in more detail in Fig. 4.

It works as follows: As input a source frame and a target frame is needed. Also the last used relative transformation is given which for the first frame is set to the identity. The output will be the optimized transformation between the two frames.

The first goal that needs to be achieved is to calculate the rigid transformation that describes the alignment of two consecutive pictures. To achieve this the depth values are used directly as a dense point cloud with information drawn from all pixels. From the RGB values sparse features are extracted at points where the images have some special attribute that can easily be recognized in the next picture. How this extraction of feature points is done exactly shall not be part of this discussion. For the interested reader however I recommend to look into SIFT [4], SURF [5] and ORB [6]. Then these points are associated with their corresponding depth values. Since these feature points are determined heuristically false matches may occur. To get these out of the equation a RANSAC algorithm is used. RANSAC stands for "random sample consensus" and can be applied to practically every experimental data set where one wants to find and eliminate outliers. In our case these datasets are our RGB-D pictures.

What RANSAC does is it that it randomly takes out three feature points from all the points found in the previous step. It then computes the optimal transformation function for these three points. After that the algorithm checks which of the remaining feature points also can (within a threshold) be correctly transformed into their corresponding coordinates in the target frame using this transformation. This is repeated for different triplets of feature points. The transformation that produces most of such so called inliers is than taken and optimized via an error metric.

4

To do so an error metric has to be defined which describes in some way the error between the picture that would emerge if one applied the current transformation to the source picture and the target picture as it really is. Then the optimized transformation can be calculated by minimizing this error over all points. Henry et al. use the error metric described in equation 1.

$$\mathbf{T}^* = \underset{\mathbf{T}}{\operatorname{argmin}} \left(\frac{1}{|A_f|} \sum_{i \in A_f} |Proj(\mathbf{T}(f_s^i)) - Proj(f_t^i)|^2 \right) \tag{1}$$

There T^* is the optimized transformation, $|A_f|$ is the number of inliers of the RANSAC algorithm. The $Proj()$ function indicates that not the 3D coordinates of the frames are used here but coordinates in pixel space. That means that the error is calculated in means of pixels with 2D pixel coordinates of the picture and one depth coordinate. $\mathbf{T}(f_s^i)$ uses the source frame f_s as input and applies to it the current estimation of the Transformation. From this the actual coordinates of the new picture f_t are subtracted. This leads to a better result then when using the more traditional euclidian error metric (see Eq. 2) which uses real 3D coordinates with a weight factor w_i.

$$\mathbf{T}^* = \underset{\mathbf{T}}{\operatorname{argmin}} \left(\frac{1}{|A_f|} \sum_{i \in A_f} w_i |\mathbf{T}(f_s^i) - f_t^i|^2 \right). \tag{2}$$

In our case that is done via two-frame sparse bundle adjustment (SBA) which I will explain later (section 4.A). In this optimization step some inliers may fall out due to the decreasing threshold. Should after all that the number of inliers be below some lower border then the whole calculation is discarded since the result is not certain enough. In that case the following step is initialized with the transformation used to align the last two frames. Otherwise we have calculated an initial estimation for the transformation.

After that the Iterative Closest Points (ICP) loop is executed. In this loop first the associations for concurrent frames of the dense point cloud are calculated. To do this the before calculated transformation is applied to the origin pixel. Based on this together with color difference and shape difference the corresponding pixel in the target frame is determined. Then the alignment error of the visual features and the dense point cloud are optimized using another error metric:

$$\mathbf{T}^* = \underset{\mathbf{T}}{\operatorname{argmin}} \left[\left(\frac{1}{|A_f|} \sum_{i \in A_f} w_i |\mathbf{T}(f_s^i) - f_t^i|^2 \right) + \beta \left(\frac{1}{|A_d|} \sum_{j \in A_d} w_j |(\mathbf{T}(p_s^j) - p_t^j) \cdot n_t^j|^2 \right) \right]. \tag{3}$$

The first part of this is the same that we used before for RANSAC, the second part uses the same mechanism but is applied to the dense point cloud, that is all pixels. n_t^j is the normal of the target point. That means that here point-to-plain distances are calculated. This makes the calculation more robust than when using point-to-point distances. This step is repeated until the error falls below a threshold or a maximum number of iterations has been reached.

Since the second step uses all available pixels instead of only some feature points it is way more expensive than the first one. Experiments though have shown that with a large number of inliers in the first step the second step only leads to a very small improvement. For this reason another threshold is implemented into the algorithm which skips the second step (ICP) if some number of inliers is reached for the first step (RANSAC). This lowers the exactness of the algorithm a little but brings a huge increase in performance.

After these steps T^* will usually be a very good approximation of the real transformation which allows the new frame to be aligned with the existent map and makes a trajectory estimation of the device possible.

B. SLAM Front-End of Endres et al. [2]

In their system Endres et al. divided their approach in an SLAM Front-end and a SLAM Back-end. The front end has the same functionality as the RGB-D ICP algorithm of Henry et al. The back end does the global alignment much like step two and three from Henry et al. This means that we will concentrate on the Front-end in this chapter.

The system is very equal to the one implemented by Henry et al. only some improvements that were made there were left out by Endres et al. They first extract feature points from the 3D point clouds as Henry et al. do. In this approach though three different feature extractors, namely SURF, SIFT and ORB, are compared which makes it interesting to us. While ORB is the newest approach and is supposed to be very fast SURF is able to dynamically adjust the number of feature points extracted to obtain stability while still keeping calculation time low if too many features can be found. As in Henry et al. these feature points then are connected with their corresponding depth values. To calculate a first estimation and at the same time coping with outliers RANSAC is performed. In this approach the euclidian error metric is used. To improve the transformation the euclidian error metric is minimized. So in this approach the whole data set never gets used. Instead the current frame is not only compared to the frame directly before but to the three most recent frames and 17 other "uniformly sampled earlier frames" [2]. This can be done in parallel. The new frame is then aligned with at least one of these frames. It is also possible to have

5

Fig. 5. example picture which shows how the weighting function operates: the darker the point the less it is taken into account for further calculation [3]

alignments with more than one previous frame. In fact this even improves the global alignment. The incorporation of older frames in this alignment process already shows that this approach relies more on the global alignment to produce valid maps than on the frame-to-frame alignment as in Henry et al. [1]

C. Visual Odometry by Audras et al. [3]

Here Audras et al. [3] try a completely different approach. They try to "avoid feature extraction and matching" [3] since errors can occur in that process. They work with a color brightness and a depth value for each pixel. For alignment a warping function is calculated for concurrent pictures. This is again done by minimizing the euclidian error. The method to do this though is very different. In this approach only the intensity is used in the process of finding a warping function. Also how the pixels which are used for calculation are chosen differs greatly from the other approaches where sparse feature points were extracted. Here the jacobian of the error function of the intensity is minimized. To do this first the intensity gradient of each pixel is calculated. Now instead of extracting feature points pixels are selected by checking for maximal gradients in all dimensions of freedom. For each dimension those pixels are chosen that have the biggest gradient in that direction. These points are used to calculate the warping function. This is done by minimizing the error function with a first order approximation. For further performance increase a multi resolution approach is implemented. That means: first a warping is calculated for a very low resolution using only a few points. Then the resolution is increased and the extra points are used to improve the warping function. The extraction of data points directly from the jacobian of the error function instead of using sparse feature points makes it possible to achieve a trajectory estimation that is very exact. Also a weight function is implemented to extract very dark pixels and other disturbing objects like people moving around from the selection process.

D. performance comparison of the different approaches

All implementations have been thoroughly tested by their creators. I will now attempt to use these test results to compare the approaches in their robustness, efficiency, accuracy and overall performance.

Henry et al. tested their system with two indoor environments both of which contain at least one big loop closure. The system "was carried by a person, and generally pointed in the direction of travel" [1]. The test data consists of about 900 and about 700 frames over a length of 71 and 114 meters. Both results are compared to way more exact models (one is obtained via a laser scanner, the other is the architectural floor plan). A first result of the experiments is that the RANSAC using the error metric in pixel space works way better than the euclidian approach. Namely the mean inliers per frame for the euclidian metric was 60.3 feature points while using the error in pixel space produced a mean of 116.7 inliers [1]. This resulted in a significantly smaller drift of the frame alignment. The measurement was done by performing SLAM over some different distances varying between $3m$ and $5.5m$. These distances were measured exactly and then compared to the SLAM results. This can be seen in Fig. 6. For testing purposes all experiments were performed once at daylight and once at night with no artificial light. We want to concentrate on the daylight results. The most important value is the error of the two-stage RGB-D ICP, since that is the complete system. For the day version this is $11 \pm 5cm$ which is identical to the result of RE-RANSAC only which is the RANSAC algorithm with the error metric in pixel space. That these two results are equal is because the RANSAC algorithm produces enough inliers in every frame for ICP to never be run at all. Also an important result ist that

6

	RE-RANSAC	EE-RANSAC	ICP	RGB-D ICP	Two-Stage RGB-D ICP
Intel-Day	0.11 (±0.05)	0.16 (±0.07)	0.15 (±0.05)	**0.10 (±0.04)**	0.11 (±0.05)
Intel-Night	1.09 (±0.88)	1.15 (±0.89)	0.17 (±0.06)	**0.15 (±0.08)**	0.15 (±0.09)

Fig. 6. Error of different methods used to measure 3-5.5m distances. Values are mean absolute errors in meters [1]

	RE-RANSAC	EE-RANSAC	ICP	RGB-D ICP	Two-Stage RGB-D ICP
Intel-Day	0.21 (±0.03)	0.20 (±0.05)	0.72 (±0.73)	0.48 (±0.10)	0.21 (±0.03)
Intel-Night	0.20 (±0.05)	0.20 (±0.05)	0.43 (±0.64)	0.57 (±0.47)	0.37 (±0.63)

Fig. 7. mean time needed for calculation per frame in a test scenario. Values are mean seconds per frame. [1]

the error with two-stage RGB-D ICP, which return the RANSAC result if a minimum number of inliers is reached, is only marginally bigger than when performing RGB-D ICP without this extra option. This legitimates the use of the two step version of the algorithm. Which is good since the use of the two-stage algorithm results in a calculation time per frame of $0.21 \pm 0.03s$ which is less than half of what is needed when performing RGB-D ICP as a whole (see Fig 7).

Endres et al. did not produce own data to test their system. Instead they used publicly available data sets so produce a comparable result. In the chosen dataset nine different indoor environments are used. The results can be seen in Fig. 8.

The team calculates an average accuracy of $9.7cm$ and 3.95 degrees. That however ist not directly comparable to the results from Henry et al. since the mean distance that has been traveled in the sequences is way bigger than $3 - 5m$. In their own evaluation Endres et al. say that rpy and xyz are very easy sequences. Still if one compares the translational root mean square error (RSME) of xyz, which is about 2cm at 7m length or maybe more realistically the dataset 360 which has an error of about 10cm on a length of 5.82m both sequences including about 800 frames. One can conclude that the accuracy of the approach from Endres et al. is a little better. In the worst case it is about equal, but in average the drift is less than $10cm$ at an average length of $10.34m$. Which results in an error of about the same size as with Henry at al. but at double mean length.

Endres et al. also compare their results among themselves using different feature extractors. As one can see in Fig. 9 SIFTGPU and SURF both produce equally accurate results and trajectory estimation is successful in all nine experimental datasets. ORB on the other hand produces translational RMSE of about double magnitude and even fails to provide enough data for two of the sequences at all so that no trajectory estimation is possible. However, if one takes a look at the time needed to calculate the feature points (see Fig. 9) it is possible to see that ORB is faster by a whole order of magnitude than SIFTGPU, which still only needs half the time of SURF. On average the whole system needs $0.35s$ per frame which is running on a quad-core CPU with 8GB memory and already sped up by parallelizing which made the process faster by a factor of 2. That means that this approach is somewhat more exact for frame to frame alignment but is significantly slower in calculation and can only be done in real time using high end hardware. This is especially valid since SIFTGPU also is about 3.5 times faster than normal, non parallelized SIFT.

Audras et al. unfortunately does not publish evaluation data in such detail. They evaluated their system by putting it on a mobile robot and as a ground truth also put a high precision laser scan system on board. Their system too works in real time.

Sequence Name	Length	Duration	Avg. Angular Velocity	Avg. Transl. Velocity	Frames	Total Runtime	g^2o Runtime	Transl. RMSE	Rot. RMSE
FR1 360	5.82 m	28.69 s	41.60 deg/s	0.21 m/s	745	145 s	0.66 s	0.103 m	3.41°
FR1 desk2	10.16 m	24.86 s	29.31 deg/s	0.43 m/s	614	176 s	0.68 s	0.102 m	3.81°
FR1 desk	9.26 m	23.40 s	23.33 deg/s	0.41 m/s	575	199 s	1.31 s	0.049 m	2.43°
FR1 floor	12.57 m	49.87 s	15.07 deg/s	0.26 m/s	1214	488 s	3.93 s	0.055 m	2.35°
FR1 plant	14.80 m	41.53 s	27.89 deg/s	0.37 m/s	1112	424 s	1.28 s	0.142 m	6.34°
FR1 room	15.99 m	48.90 s	29.88 deg/s	0.33 m/s	1332	423 s	1.56 s	0.219 m	9.04°
FR1 rpy	1.66 m	27.67 s	50.15 deg/s	0.06 m/s	687	243 s	10.26 s	0.042 m	2.50°
FR1 teddy	15.71 m	50.82 s	21.32 deg/s	0.32 m/s	1395	556 s	1.72 s	0.138 m	4.75°
FR1 xyz	7.11 m	30.09 s	8.92 deg/s	0.24 m/s	788	365 s	40.09 s	0.021 m	0.90°

Fig. 8. evaluation data from nine different input sequences. [2]

7

	Success	Transl. RMSE (Avg. ± Std. Dev.)	Rot. RMSE (Avg. ± Std. Dev.)	Type	Count Avg. ± Std. Dev.	Runtime Detection + Extraction Avg. ± Std. Dev.
SIFTGPU	9/9	0.097 m ± 0.063 m	3.95°± 2.47°	SURF	1733 ± 153	0.34 s + 0.34 s
SURF	9/9	0.098 m ± 0.078 m	3.39°± 1.55°	ORB	1117 ± 558	0.018 s + 0.0086 s
ORB	7/9	0.215 m ± 0.189 m	7.75°± 5.55°	SIFTGPU	1918 ± 599	0.19 s

Fig. 9. Evaluation of the different feature detectors. Error and success rate on the left, count and mean calculation time on the right. [2]

Fig. 10. Experimental results of the trajectory estimation of the laser scanner in red and the corresponding estimations of the RGB-D SLAM system in blue. [3]

Their algorithm was even only running on a laptop which is likely to have way less power than the machine that Endres et al. used. However in the experiment in some situations there were problems because the computer was too slow. Audras et al. claim that "the bottle neck was due to the bandwidth of the laptop hard-drive which was saving additional data for analysis and presentation of the results." [3] It is unclear though if the problems would vanish if the additional data is not collected. From Fig. 10 one can see that the RGB-D SLAM system collects a lot of drift during the second bend. That, according to the authors, is due to the fact that the robot took the bend too fast and therefore the overlap from picture to picture was too small for an exact evaluation.

In addition Audras et al. observed a drift of $1m$ at a length of $50m$. Based on a linear accumulation of drift this would mean that the accuracy of this approach is significantly worse than the other two. However it is more likely that with double length the error increases more than double since a small error in the angular estimation at the beginning can result in a bigger error later. Therefore, although with great incertitude, I conclude that the approach from Audras et al. propably has about the same accuracy as the other two, at least one of the same magnitude.

So over all the approaches all have an error of about equal magnitude which varies a lot more from scenery to scenery than from approach to approach. Also all systems are able to calculate the frame to frame alignment in real time which also is an important accomplishment.

IV. GLOBAL MAP ALIGNMENT

The frame to frame alignment that is performed for every frame is a good method to build maps of a limited size. If bigger maps are to be produced without loosing accuracy global alignment methods are needed since otherwise the accumulated errors of each frame alignment may result in a large deviation from the real world. In the worst case, if the camera returns to a position that has been visited before but the accumulated error estimates the position wrong, there are two representations of the same region in different locations" [1]. To avoid such errors many approaches have incorporated global optimization tools within their systems.

A. global optimization from Henry et al. [1]

Henry et al. implemented a loop closure detection. The easiest way to implement this would be to use RANSAC and just apply it to every previous frame. Obviously that is not an efficient approach and after only a few seconds the calculation needed would make a real time processing impossible. To be able to perform loop closure detection without increasing the calculation effort with each additional frame Henry et al. introduce keyframes. Only the keyframes (or a subset of those) are then checked via RANSAC if a loop closure can be found. This is again improved by not only taking every n-th frame as a keyframe. Instead a new keyframe is selected whenever the overlap of the current frame with the last keyframe is below a threshold. This approach was implemented in a previous version of the system. In the current version Henry et al. improved again by establishing a new keyframe whenever "the accumulated rotation or translation is above a threshold." [1] Only these keyframes are then used to search for loop closures. This search is triggered every time a new keyframe is selected. To still reduce the number of frames to run RANSAC on, only keyframes within some radius of the currently estimated global position are taken into account. For further performance improvement place recognition is used which allows keyframes to be rapidly compared by storing feature descriptors of each keyframe which can be compared very fast.

Another method used to optimize global alignment is pose graph optimization. This method represents each frame as a node of a graph and introduces edges between nodes if some constraints can be found between these frames. So before loop closure the graph looks like a chain. With a loop closure new constraints can be added to old frames. To minimize conflict Henry et al. use TORO which edit the vertices which "are parameterized by translation and rotation components" [1].

Additionally sparse bundle adjustment is used to minimize drift. This method minimizes the re-projection error. That is the error if one takes the 3D points that have been calculated and stored into the internal map and re-project these into the pixel representation of the camera. The sum of the error of this re-projection is then minimized resulting in more accurate frame alignment. For this process all inliers of the RANSAC algorithm are used. Therefore the question arises what to do if RANSAC failed and the alignment was done solely by ICP. To solve this problem new pairs of points have to be created. This is done by sampling points "from one of the frames across a grid in image space". Then the closest point in the corresponding frame is found by using the transformation calculated from ICP. Only pairs with a distance lower than some threshold are kept. Also the corresponding normals may only deviate by some angle. The remaining points are our feature point equivalents.

B. SLAM Back-end by Endres et al. [2]

Endres et al. use a pose graph for global optimization where the transformations calculated by the front end form the edges of the graph. Remember that RANSAC was applied to 20 different frames and the new frame possibly gets aligned according to more than one frame. So in the pose graph the new frame is not necessarily only adjacent to the most recent frame but might also be to any of the other 19 frames which RANSAC is performed. Due to errors this pose graph is not globally consistent. Here the g^2o-framework is used to optimize this graph. [7] To do this again an error function is minimized. For further details of this function and how to minimize the error see [Kruemmerle et al. [7]].

Unfortunately Endres et al. do not explicitly explain their loop closure detection. It is implemented though by applying RANSAC to 17 evenly distributed previous frames. Endres et al. optimize through the pose graph, but also claim that "global optimization is especially beneficial in case of a loop closure" [2].

C. performance comparison and evaluation

Henry et al. focus on the comparison of a sparse bundle adjustment (SBA) approach and a pose graph approach which is optimized by a framework called TORO. This evaluation is mainly done qualitatively. That means that not a lot of numbers are compared this time but results are compared with images.

In Fig. 11 a optimization has been performed from the same experimental data after loop closure occurred. It is easy to see which method works better here. SBA produces a very linearly looking trajectory estimation that only has deviated a little from the original estimation. TORO on the other hand has failed to incorporate the loop closure constraints in a consistent way into the rest of the data. The result is a trajectory estimation that deviates a lot from what the actual trajectory looked like.

The down side of this is that SBA does need a lot more calculation time which also increases a lot with the number of frames that has to be handled (see Fig 12).

The evaluation of the pose graph optimization from Endres et al. unfortunately is very short. They only claim that for small graphs it can be done in real time even for every frame. This could be extended to larger graphs by not performing optimization on every frame. This probably would break down though if a loop closure is detected since as we have seen at Henry et al. a non linear constraint in the pose graph takes a lot more time to incorporate. Still Endres et al. say that "the ratio of graph optimization versus the total runtime was below 6%." [2]

Since my third source does not even implement a global optimization at all there also is no evaluation to do.

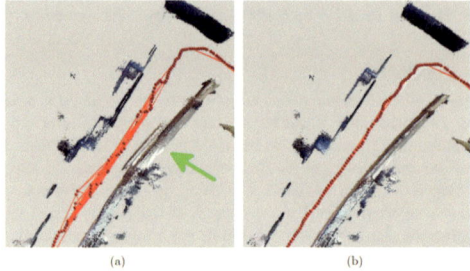

(a)   (b)

Fig. 11. globally optimized trajectory after a loop closure has been found (a) via pose graph optimization (TORO) (b) via SBA [1]

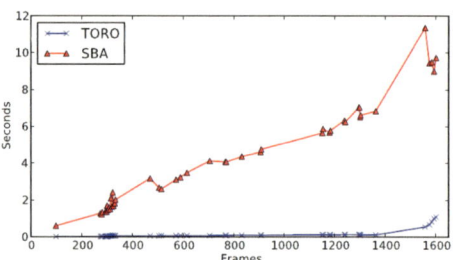

Fig. 12. time needed for global optimization in seconds depending on the number of frames [1]

We still can see from the comparison within Henry et al. that SBA will produce better results but at the cost that global optimization can probably not be performed in real time. With the pose graph optimization approach at least for small and middle sized mappings real time calculation is possible. On the other hand the accuracy might be quite bad if a loop closure is detected which can not be incorporated consistently into the previous map. That is very bad since loop closures are needed when mapping big environments to be able to get rid of accumulated drift and thereby get a consistent global mapping.

V. INTERNAL MAP REPRESENTATION

Since each frame "gives us roughly 250,000 points" [1] and we have 30 frames per second it is necessary for the internal representation to in some way compress this data without loosing too much information. One could for example down sample the internal map to a lower pixel resolution. This would however result into loss of accuracy and information loss. Therefore other ideas have been developed and implemented that can store a map incorporating information from all pixels without having to build the map from many millions of them.

A. surfel representation

Henry et al. [1] use what they call "surfel representation" [1]. It contains "a location, a surface orientation, a patch size and a color" [1]. This means that this is in fact a two dimensional pixel placed in a 3D environment. Initially for each pixel a surfel is created. These surfels are then added, removed or updated with regards to further frames and their incorporation into the scenery. To ensure an improving process each surfel gets a measure of confidence which indicates how certain the surfel is. This measure increases if the same surfel can be identified from different pictures and different angles. With this technique surfels that came into existence due to some error as moving things or bad lighting can be removed after the same location has been seen from other angles. Other surfels get updated and with this process become more and more exact not only in location and color but also its orientation and size can be refined.

The surfel representation of the map currently is not done in real time with the other calculations but as a post process from point cloud maps. The main reason for that is that the whole map needs to be rebuild whenever a global optimization changes all camera pose estimations.

10

B. 3D occupancy grid maps

Endres et al. use OctoMap [8], which is a "octree-based mapping framework" [2]. A octree is a tree data structure where every node represents a cubic space within the internal map. With the tree structure this voxel can be divided into smaller voxels making a multi resolution approach possible. So in that representation voxels are used instead of surfels. Meaning not only a surface is build but instead 3D elements are used to form the surrounding. The main benefit of this 3D representation is that one can not only map where objects are but also incorporate free space explicitly. That is a very useful thing for many applications, above all for robot navigation. OctoMap also marks unexplored ares as such and also incorporates updatability wich is performed in a probabilistic way. That is about the same as the confidence level introduces at Henry et al. [1].

VI. CONCLUSION AND OUTLOOK

Overall one can conclude that RGB-D SLAM systems are now able to produce 3D maps of large scale indoor environments of an acceptable quality even with low cost equipment. The introduction of Kinect style cameras has made it possible for many researchers to contribute to the development of RGB-D SLAM systems. Now highly developed systems are able to calculate quite accurate 3D maps of indoor environments using a lot of optimization tools and refinements of traditional techniques. Though these refinements mean a lot of extra calculating the systems have been optimized to a point where all calculation can be done in real time. This means that now researchers are at a point where real challenges can be tackled with RGB-D SLAM systems. This could mean improved robot navigation, and maybe even more important: dense mapping of indoor environments. Since that is an application which not only researchers could use. First approaches exist which try to make the 3D modeling process interactive and consumer usable. This could mean that in the near future systems are developed and distributed that are able to perform 3D modeling even of very large indoor environments as a novice user. This could for example be used in real estate. There the technique makes it possible to easily and at low cost create 3D maps of flats and houses and make these available for customers over the internet. RGB-D SLAM systems therefore will sure be further improved and refined. But with the real time calculation speed an important limitation has already been cracked. The next challenge will be to make the systems available to not only a large range of researcher but also to consumers in many areas.

REFERENCES

[1] P. Henry, M. Krainin, E. Herbst, X. Ren, and D. Fox, "RGB-D mapping: Using Kinect-style depth cameras for dense 3D modeling of indoor environments," *International Journal of Robotics Research.*

[2] F. Endres, J. Hess, N. Engelhard, J. Sturm, D. Cremers, and W. Burgard, "An Evaluation of the RGB-D SLAM System," *Proc. of the IEEE Int. Conf. on Robotics and Automation (ICRA).*

[3] C. Audras, A. I. Comport, M. Meilland, and P. Rives, "Real-time dense appearance-based SLAM for RGB-D sensors," *Australian Conference on Robotics and Automation.*

[4] D. Lowe, "Discriminative image features from scale-invariant keypoints," *International Journal of Computer Vision*, vol. 60, no. 2, pp. 91–110, 2004.

[5] H. Bay, A. Ess, T. Tuytelaars, and L. V. Gool, "Speeded-up robust features (SURF)," *Comput. Vis. Image Underst.*, vol. 110.

[6] E. Rublee, V. Rabaud, K. Konolige, and G. Bradski, "ORB: an efficient alternative to SIFT or SURF," *Proc. of the IEEE Intl. Conf. on Computer Vision (ICCV)*, vol. 13.

[7] R. Kuemmerle, G. Grisetti, H. Strasdat, K. Konolige, and W. Burgard, "g2o: A general framework for graph optimization," *Proc. of the IEEE Intl. Conf. on Robotics and Automation (ICRA).*

[8] K. Wurm, A. Hornung, M. Bennewitz, C. Stachiniss, and W. Burgrad, "OctoMap: A probabilistic, flexible, and compact 3D map representation for robotic systems," *Proc. of the ICRA.*